The Bible tells us that God made everything. In **Genesis 1:31** it says that God saw everything that God had made, and it was very good! God thinks the world (including you and me!) is beautiful. **Psalm 34:8** says "taste and see that God is good." Look around yourself right now, and see some beautiful things that God made.

Thank you, God, for making _____

<u>You</u> can practice being God's paintbrush!

Make some edible art using a simple sugar cookie recipe or purchase refrigerated cookie dough. Make "paint" by mixing two egg yolks and 1/2 tsp. water. Divide into small cups. Add a few drops of food color to each one. Roll out cookies, cut with cookie cutters, and place on cookie sheet. Using a clean paintbrush, draw pictures and designs, and/or write words on the cookies. Bake for six to ten minutes; watch carefully, and remove them before they brown.

Taste and see that God is good! How is that like being God's paintbrush?

A sunbeam peeked in my window this morning, and painted a rainbow on my wall.

I think the sunbeam is God's paintbrush dipped in a watercolor sea, painting clouds and coloring our world.

What color would you paint the world today?

Use a prism to create rainbows (sometimes a piece of crystal or even plastic can work). Move it around and watch the rainbows dance on different things.

 Look at God's creation in different ways. Use a magnifying glass or microscope to make tiny things bigger. Use a telescope or binoculars to bring far away things closer. Use a kaleidoscope, a dragonfly eye, or colored glasses to see things differently. What new things do you notice?

Look in a mirror (a big floor-length one if you have one). What do you see? Make some different faces. Which faces do you like best?

In September, a new boy came to school. During recess, nobody picked him for the soccer team.
    At lunch, he ate all by himself.

What I remember most about him were his eyes.
    They looked sad.

My teacher had us all do a mural one day. The new boy helped me draw a lion. He is a great artist.
    Maybe we will be friends.

My teacher watched us working together. What I remember most about my teacher were her eyes.
    They looked happy.

Today our school went for a hike.
The sky looked like a lemon meringue pie.
The fields of flowers seemed like layers
of orange, red and purple jelly beans.

The vines looked just like a giant jump rope
and the hills like big slippery slides.
The branches of the trees
made a fantastic jungle gym.

I wonder if God likes lemon meringue pie
and jelly beans — just like me.

The Bible tells us that God made everything. In **Genesis 1:31** it says that God saw everything that God had made, and it was very good! God thinks the world (including you and me!) is beautiful. **Psalm 34:8** says "taste and see that God is good." Look around yourself right now, and see some beautiful things that God made.

Thank you, God, for making _____

You can practice being God's paintbrush!

Make some edible art using a simple sugar cookie recipe or purchase refrigerated cookie dough. Make "paint" by mixing two egg yolks and 1/2 tsp. water. Divide into small cups. Add a few drops of food color to each one. Roll out cookies, cut with cookie cutters, and place on cookie sheet. Using a clean paintbrush, draw pictures and designs, and/or write words on the cookies. Bake for six to ten minutes; watch carefully, and remove them before they brown.

**Taste and see that God is good!
How is that like being God's paintbrush?**

A sunbeam peeked in my window this morning, and painted a rainbow on my wall.

I think the sunbeam is God's paintbrush dipped in a watercolor sea, painting clouds and coloring our world.

What color would you paint the world today?

Use a prism to create rainbows (sometimes a piece of crystal or even plastic can work). Move it around and watch the rainbows dance on different things.

Look at God's creation in different ways. Use a magnifying glass or microscope to make tiny things bigger. Use a telescope or binoculars to bring far away things closer. Use a kaleidoscope, a dragonfly eye, or colored glasses to see things differently. What new things do you notice?

Look in a mirror (a big floor-length one if you have one). What do you see? Make some different faces. Which faces do you like best?

In September, a new boy came to school.
During recess, nobody picked him
for the soccer team.
    At lunch, he ate all by himself.

What I remember most about him
were his eyes.
    They looked sad.

My teacher had us all do a mural one day.
The new boy helped me draw a lion.
He is a great artist.
    Maybe we will be friends.

My teacher watched
us working together.
What I remember most about
my teacher were her eyes.
    They looked happy.

Today our school went for a hike.
The sky looked like a lemon meringue pie.
The fields of flowers seemed like layers
of orange, red and purple jelly beans.

The vines looked just like a giant jump rope
and the hills like big slippery slides.
The branches of the trees
made a fantastic jungle gym.

I wonder if God likes lemon meringue pie
and jelly beans — just like me.

Seeing

The Bible tells us that God made everything. In **Genesis 1:31** it says that God saw everything that God had made, and it was very good! God thinks the world (including you and me!) is beautiful. **Psalm 34:8** says "taste and see that God is good." Look around yourself right now, and see some beautiful things that God made.

Thank you, God, for making _____

You can practice being God's paintbrush!

Make some edible art using a simple sugar cookie recipe or purchase refrigerated cookie dough. Make "paint" by mixing two egg yolks and 1/2 tsp. water. Divide into small cups. Add a few drops of food color to each one. Roll out cookies, cut with cookie cutters, and place on cookie sheet. Using a clean paintbrush, draw pictures and designs, and/or write words on the cookies. Bake for six to ten minutes; watch carefully, and remove them before they brown.

Taste and see that God is good! How is that like being God's paintbrush?

A sunbeam peeked in my window this morning, and painted a rainbow on my wall.

I think the sunbeam is God's paintbrush dipped in a watercolor sea, painting clouds and coloring our world.

What color would you paint the world today?

Use a prism to create rainbows (sometimes a piece of crystal or even plastic can work). Move it around and watch the rainbows dance on different things.

In September, a new boy came to school.
During recess, nobody picked him
for the soccer team.
 At lunch, he ate all by himself.

What I remember most about him
were his eyes.
 They looked sad.

My teacher had us all do a mural one day.
The new boy helped me draw a lion.
He is a great artist.
 Maybe we will be friends.

My teacher watched
us working together.
What I remember most about
my teacher were her eyes.
 They looked happy.

Look at God's creation in different ways. Use a magnifying glass or microscope to make tiny things bigger. Use a telescope or binoculars to bring far away things closer. Use a kaleidoscope, a dragonfly eye, or colored glasses to see things differently. What new things do you notice?

Look in a mirror (a big floor-length one if you have one). What do you see? Make some different faces. Which faces do you like best?

Today our school went for a hike.
The sky looked like a lemon meringue pie.
The fields of flowers seemed like layers
of orange, red and purple jelly beans.

The vines looked just like a giant jump rope
and the hills like big slippery slides.
The branches of the trees
made a fantastic jungle gym.

I wonder if God likes lemon meringue pie
and jelly beans — just like me.

The Bible tells us that God made everything. In **Genesis 1:31** it says that God saw everything that God had made, and it was very good! God thinks the world (including you and me!) is beautiful. **Psalm 34:8** says "taste and see that God is good." Look around yourself right now, and see some beautiful things that God made.

Thank you, God, for making _____

You can practice being God's paintbrush!

Make some edible art using a simple sugar cookie recipe or purchase refrigerated cookie dough. Make "paint" by mixing two egg yolks and 1/2 tsp. water. Divide into small cups. Add a few drops of food color to each one. Roll out cookies, cut with cookie cutters, and place on cookie sheet. Using a clean paintbrush, draw pictures and designs, and/or write words on the cookies. Bake for six to ten minutes; watch carefully, and remove them before they brown.

Taste and see that God is good! How is that like being God's paintbrush?

A sunbeam peeked in my window this morning, and painted a rainbow on my wall.

I think the sunbeam is God's paintbrush dipped in a watercolor sea, painting clouds and coloring our world.

What color would you paint the world today?

Use a prism to create rainbows (sometimes a piece of crystal or even plastic can work). Move it around and watch the rainbows dance on different things.

 **Look at God's creation in different ways.** Use a magnifying glass or microscope to make tiny things bigger. Use a telescope or binoculars to bring far away things closer. Use a kaleidoscope, a dragonfly eye, or colored glasses to see things differently. What new things do you notice?

Look in a mirror (a big floor-length one if you have one). What do you see? Make some different faces. Which faces do you like best?

In September, a new boy came to school.
During recess, nobody picked him
for the soccer team.
    At lunch, he ate all by himself.

What I remember most about him
were his eyes.
    They looked sad.

My teacher had us all do a mural one day.
The new boy helped me draw a lion.
He is a great artist.
    Maybe we will be friends.

My teacher watched
us working together.
What I remember most about
my teacher were her eyes.
    They looked happy.

Today our school went for a hike.
The sky looked like a lemon meringue pie.
The fields of flowers seemed like layers
of orange, red and purple jelly beans.

The vines looked just like a giant jump rope
and the hills like big slippery slides.
The branches of the trees
made a fantastic jungle gym.

I wonder if God likes lemon meringue pie
and jelly beans — just like me.

The Bible tells us that God made everything. In **Genesis 1:31** it says that God saw everything that God had made, and it was very good! God thinks the world (including you and me!) is beautiful. **Psalm 34:8** says "taste and see that God is good." Look around yourself right now, and see some beautiful things that God made.

hank you, God, for making _____

You can practice being God's paintbrush!

Make some edible art using a simple sugar cookie recipe or purchase refrigerated cookie dough. Make "paint" by mixing two egg yolks and 1/2 tsp. water. Divide into small cups. Add a few drops of food color to each one. Roll out cookies, cut with cookie cutters, and place on cookie sheet. Using a clean paintbrush, draw pictures and designs, and/or write words on the cookies. Bake for six to ten minutes; watch carefully, and remove them before they brown.

Taste and see that God is good! How is that like being God's paintbrush?

A sunbeam peeked in my window this morning, and painted a rainbow on my wall.

I think the sunbeam is God's paintbrush dipped in a watercolor sea, painting clouds and coloring our world.

What color would you paint the world today?

Use a prism to create rainbows (sometimes a piece of crystal or even plastic can work). Move it around and watch the rainbows dance on different things.

In September, a new boy came to school.
During recess, nobody picked him
for the soccer team.
    At lunch, he ate all by himself.

What I remember most about him
were his eyes.
    They looked sad.

My teacher had us all do a mural one day.
The new boy helped me draw a lion.
He is a great artist.
    Maybe we will be friends.

My teacher watched
us working together.
What I remember most about
my teacher were her eyes.
    They looked happy.

Look at God's creation in different ways. Use a magnifying glass or microscope to make tiny things bigger. Use a telescope or binoculars to bring far away things closer. Use a kaleidoscope, a dragonfly eye, or colored glasses to see things differently. What new things do you notice?

Look in a mirror (a big floor-length one if you have one). What do you see? Make some different faces. Which faces do you like best?

Today our school went for a hike.
The sky looked like a lemon meringue pie.
The fields of flowers seemed like layers
of orange, red and purple jelly beans.

The vines looked just like a giant jump rope
and the hills like big slippery slides.
The branches of the trees
made a fantastic jungle gym.

I wonder if God likes lemon meringue pie
and jelly beans — just like me.

The Bible tells us that God made everything. In **Genesis 1:31** it says that God saw everything that God had made, and it was very good! God thinks the world (including you and me!) is beautiful. **Psalm 34:8** says "taste and see that God is good." Look around yourself right now, and see some beautiful things that God made.

Thank you, God, for making _____

You can practice being God's paintbrush!

Make some edible art using a simple sugar cookie recipe or purchase refrigerated cookie dough. Make "paint" by mixing two egg yolks and 1/2 tsp. water. Divide into small cups. Add a few drops of food color to each one. Roll out cookies, cut with cookie cutters, and place on cookie sheet. Using a clean paintbrush, draw pictures and designs, and/or write words on the cookies. Bake for six to ten minutes; watch carefully, and remove them before they brown.

Taste and see that God is good! How is that like being God's paintbrush?

A sunbeam peeked in my window this morning, and painted a rainbow on my wall.

I think the sunbeam is God's paintbrush dipped in a watercolor sea, painting clouds and coloring our world.

What color would you paint the world today?

Use a prism to create rainbows (sometimes a piece of crystal or even plastic can work). Move it around and watch the rainbows dance on different things.

Look at God's creation in different ways. Use a magnifying glass or microscope to make tiny things bigger. Use a telescope or binoculars to bring far away things closer. Use a kaleidoscope, a dragonfly eye, or colored glasses to see things differently. What new things do you notice?

Look in a mirror (a big floor-length one if you have one). What do you see? Make some different faces. Which faces do you like best?

In September, a new boy came to school. During recess, nobody picked him for the soccer team.
    At lunch, he ate all by himself.

What I remember most about him were his eyes.
    They looked sad.

My teacher had us all do a mural one day. The new boy helped me draw a lion. He is a great artist.
    Maybe we will be friends.

My teacher watched us working together. What I remember most about my teacher were her eyes.
    They looked happy.

Today our school went for a hike. The sky looked like a lemon meringue pie. The fields of flowers seemed like layers of orange, red and purple jelly beans.

The vines looked just like a giant jump rope and the hills like big slippery slides. The branches of the trees made a fantastic jungle gym.

I wonder if God likes lemon meringue pie and jelly beans — just like me.

The Bible tells us that God made everything. In **Genesis 1:31** it says that God saw everything that God had made, and it was very good! God thinks the world (including you and me!) is beautiful. **Psalm 34:8** says "taste and see that God is good." Look around yourself right now, and see some beautiful things that God made.

Thank you, God, for making _____

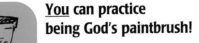

You can practice being God's paintbrush!

Make some edible art using a simple sugar cookie recipe or purchase refrigerated cookie dough. Make "paint" by mixing two egg yolks and 1/2 tsp. water. Divide into small cups. Add a few drops of food color to each one. Roll out cookies, cut with cookie cutters, and place on cookie sheet. Using a clean paintbrush, draw pictures and designs, and/or write words on the cookies. Bake for six to ten minutes; watch carefully, and remove them before they brown.

Taste and see that God is good! How is that like being God's paintbrush?

A sunbeam peeked in my window this morning, and painted a rainbow on my wall.

I think the sunbeam is God's paintbrush dipped in a watercolor sea, painting clouds and coloring our world.

What color would you paint the world today?

Use a prism to create rainbows (sometimes a piece of crystal or even plastic can work). Move it around and watch the rainbows dance on different things.

Look at God's creation in different ways. Use a magnifying glass or microscope to make tiny things bigger. Use a telescope or binoculars to bring far away things closer. Use a kaleidoscope, a dragonfly eye, or colored glasses to see things differently. What new things do you notice?

 **Look in a mirror (a big floor-length one if you have one). What do you see? Make some different faces. Which faces do you like best?**

In September, a new boy came to school. During recess, nobody picked him for the soccer team.
    At lunch, he ate all by himself.

What I remember most about him were his eyes.
    They looked sad.

My teacher had us all do a mural one day. The new boy helped me draw a lion. He is a great artist.
    Maybe we will be friends.

My teacher watched us working together. What I remember most about my teacher were her eyes.
    They looked happy.

Today our school went for a hike.
The sky looked like a lemon meringue pie.
The fields of flowers seemed like layers
of orange, red and purple jelly beans.

The vines looked just like a giant jump rope
and the hills like big slippery slides.
The branches of the trees
made a fantastic jungle gym.

I wonder if God likes lemon meringue pie
and jelly beans — just like me.

The Bible tells us that God made everything. In **Genesis 1:31** it says that God saw everything that God had made, and it was very good! God thinks the world (including you and me!) is beautiful. **Psalm 34:8** says "taste and see that God is good." Look around yourself right now, and see some beautiful things that God made.

Thank you, God, for making _____

You can practice being God's paintbrush!

Make some edible art using a simple sugar cookie recipe or purchase refrigerated cookie dough. Make "paint" by mixing two egg yolks and 1/2 tsp. water. Divide into small cups. Add a few drops of food color to each one. Roll out cookies, cut with cookie cutters, and place on cookie sheet. Using a clean paintbrush, draw pictures and designs, and/or write words on the cookies. Bake for six to ten minutes; watch carefully, and remove them before they brown.

Taste and see that God is good! How is that like being God's paintbrush?

A sunbeam peeked in my window this morning, and painted a rainbow on my wall.

I think the sunbeam is God's paintbrush dipped in a watercolor sea, painting clouds and coloring our world.

What color would you paint the world today?

Use a prism to create rainbows (sometimes a piece of crystal or even plastic can work). Move it around and watch the rainbows dance on different things.

Look at God's creation in different ways. Use a magnifying glass or microscope to make tiny things bigger. Use a telescope or binoculars to bring far away things closer. Use a kaleidoscope, a dragonfly eye, or colored glasses to see things differently. What new things do you notice?

Look in a mirror (a big floor-length one if you have one). What do you see? Make some different faces. Which faces do you like best?

In September, a new boy came to school. During recess, nobody picked him for the soccer team.
> At lunch, he ate all by himself.

What I remember most about him were his eyes.
> They looked sad.

My teacher had us all do a mural one day. The new boy helped me draw a lion. He is a great artist.
> Maybe we will be friends.

My teacher watched us working together. What I remember most about my teacher were her eyes.
> They looked happy.

Today our school went for a hike.
The sky looked like a lemon meringue pie.
The fields of flowers seemed like layers
of orange, red and purple jelly beans.

The vines looked just like a giant jump rope
and the hills like big slippery slides.
The branches of the trees
made a fantastic jungle gym.

I wonder if God likes lemon meringue pie
and jelly beans — just like me.

I wonder if God has eyes.
If so, they must be just like my teacher's.
They see when people are sad or happy.

If you saw the world through God's eyes, what would you see?

Sometimes my parents tell me
to eat more green vegetables
and fewer jelly beans!

Maybe they are right, but I still like
pink lemonade jelly beans the best.

I wonder if God likes to play.
Sometimes grown-ups don't want
to play because they are too busy
or too tired.
    I think that makes God sad.
    I think God likes me to play.

Who is in your favorite playground?

How do you play in God's playground?

If I saw the world through God's eyes, I would see _____

_____

_____

_____

Lie down on a big sheet of paper (you might have to tape some sheets of paper together). Have someone trace around your body with a pencil. Finish the drawing of yourself with markers or crayons; cut it out and put it on the wall, or give it to someone you love.

Often we find God in other people.
When we do something loving for another person, it's like we're seeing God.
We can be God's paintbrushes by coloring the world with God's love.

Sometimes I like to play
hide and seek with my friends.
We count to ten
and then start looking.
But today my friends
got tired of looking,
and went away before
they found me.
    I felt very lonely.

On Monday, I broke my Mom's vase.
I was scared.
I hid behind the large sofa
in our living room.
Mom came home.
I was glad when she found me.
    I felt lonely all by myself.

Sometimes I think God hides,
and we don't want to look for God,
because we are too busy or too afraid.

    God must feel
    terribly lonely then, too.

Where would you look for God?

God is between us, all around us, within us.

Play a game of hide and seek with a twist: one person hides, and everyone goes looking for her/him. Each person who finds her/him stays in the hiding place. Eventually, everyone is "found" together.

I "find" God in _____

I "see" God in _____

I wonder if God has eyes.
If so, they must be just like my teacher's.
They see when people are sad or happy.

If you saw the world through God's eyes, what would you see?

Sometimes my parents tell me to eat more green vegetables and fewer jelly beans!

Maybe they are right, but I still like pink lemonade jelly beans the best.

I wonder if God likes to play. Sometimes grown-ups don't want to play because they are too busy or too tired.
I think that makes God sad.
I think God likes me to play.

Who is in your favorite playground?

How do you play in God's playground?

If I saw the world through God's eyes, I would see _____

_____

_____

_____

 Lie down on a big sheet of paper (you might have to tape some sheets of paper together). Have someone trace around your body with a pencil. Finish the drawing of yourself with markers or crayons; cut it out and put it on the wall, or give it to someone you love.

Often we find God in other people.
When we do something loving for another person, it's like we're seeing God.
We can be God's paintbrushes by coloring the world with God's love.

Sometimes I like to play
hide and seek with my friends.
We count to ten
and then start looking.
But today my friends
got tired of looking,
and went away before
they found me.
    I felt very lonely.

On Monday, I broke my Mom's vase.
I was scared.
I hid behind the large sofa
in our living room.
Mom came home.
I was glad when she found me.
    I felt lonely all by myself.

Sometimes I think God hides,
and we don't want to look for God,
because we are too busy or too afraid.

    God must feel
    terribly lonely then, too.

Where would you look for God?

God is between us, all around us, within us.

Play a game of hide and seek with a twist: one person hides, and everyone goes looking for her/him. Each person who finds her/him stays in the hiding place. Eventually, everyone is "found" together.

I "find" God in _____

I "see" God in _____

SAVE THE ENVIRONMENT

I wonder if God has eyes.
If so, they must be just like my teacher's.
They see when people are sad or happy.

If you saw the world through God's eyes, what would you see?

Sometimes my parents tell me
to eat more green vegetables
and fewer jelly beans!

Maybe they are right, but I still like
pink lemonade jelly beans the best.

I wonder if God likes to play.
Sometimes grown-ups don't want
to play because they are too busy
or too tired.
I think that makes God sad.
I think God likes me to play.

Who is in your favorite playground?

How do you play in God's playground?

If I saw the world through God's eyes, I would see _____

_____

_____

_____

 Lie down on a big sheet of paper (you might have to tape some sheets of paper together). Have someone trace around your body with a pencil. Finish the drawing of yourself with markers or crayons; cut it out and put it on the wall, or give it to someone you love.

Often we find God in other people.
When we do something loving for another person, it's like we're seeing God.
We can be God's paintbrushes by coloring the world with God's love.

Sometimes I like to play
hide and seek with my friends.
We count to ten
and then start looking.
But today my friends
got tired of looking,
and went away before
they found me.
  I felt very lonely.

On Monday, I broke my Mom's vase.
I was scared.
I hid behind the large sofa
in our living room.
Mom came home.
I was glad when she found me.
  I felt lonely all by myself.

Sometimes I think God hides,
and we don't want to look for God,
because we are too busy or too afraid.

God must feel
terribly lonely then, too.

Where would you look for God?

God is between us, all around us, within us.

Play a game of hide and seek with a twist: one person hides, and everyone goes looking for her/him. Each person who finds her/him stays in the hiding place. Eventually, everyone is "found" together.

I "find" God in _____

I "see" God in _____

I wonder if God has eyes.
If so, they must be just like my teacher's.
They see when people are sad or happy.

If you saw the world through God's eyes, what would you see?

Sometimes my parents tell me to eat more green vegetables and fewer jelly beans!

Maybe they are right, but I still like pink lemonade jelly beans the best.

I wonder if God likes to play. Sometimes grown-ups don't want to play because they are too busy or too tired.
I think that makes God sad.
I think God likes me to play.

Who is in your favorite playground?

How do you play in God's playground?

If I saw the world through God's eyes, I would see _____

_____

_____

_____

Lie down on a big sheet of paper (you might have to tape some sheets of paper together). Have someone trace around your body with a pencil. Finish the drawing of yourself with markers or crayons; cut it out and put it on the wall, or give it to someone you love.

Often we find God in other people.
When we do something loving for another person, it's like we're seeing God.
We can be God's paintbrushes by coloring the world with God's love.

Sometimes I like to play
hide and seek with my friends.
We count to ten
and then start looking.
But today my friends
got tired of looking,
and went away before
they found me.
        I felt very lonely.

On Monday, I broke my Mom's vase.
I was scared.
I hid behind the large sofa
in our living room.
Mom came home.
I was glad when she found me.
        I felt lonely all by myself.

Sometimes I think God hides,
and we don't want to look for God,
because we are too busy or too afraid.

        God must feel
        terribly lonely then, too.

Where would you look for God?

God is between us, all around us, within us.

Play a game of hide and seek with a twist: one person hides, and everyone
goes looking for her/him. Each person who finds her/him stays in the hiding
place. Eventually, everyone is "found" together.

I "find" God in _____

I "see" God in _____

I wonder if God has eyes.
If so, they must be just like my teacher's.
They see when people are sad or happy.

If you saw the world through God's eyes, what would you see?

Sometimes my parents tell me to eat more green vegetables and fewer jelly beans!

Maybe they are right, but I still like pink lemonade jelly beans the best.

I wonder if God likes to play. Sometimes grown-ups don't want to play because they are too busy or too tired.
I think that makes God sad.
I think God likes me to play.

Who is in your favorite playground?

How do you play in God's playground?

If I saw the world through God's eyes, I would see _____

_____

_____

_____

Lie down on a big sheet of paper (you might have to tape some sheets of paper together). Have someone trace around your body with a pencil. Finish the drawing of yourself with markers or crayons; cut it out and put it on the wall, or give it to someone you love.

Often we find God in other people.
When we do something loving for another person, it's like we're seeing God.
We can be God's paintbrushes by coloring the world with God's love.

Sometimes I like to play
hide and seek with my friends.
We count to ten
and then start looking.
But today my friends
got tired of looking,
and went away before
they found me.
    I felt very lonely.

On Monday, I broke my Mom's vase.
I was scared.
I hid behind the large sofa
in our living room.
Mom came home.
I was glad when she found me.
    I felt lonely all by myself.

Sometimes I think God hides,
and we don't want to look for God,
because we are too busy or too afraid.

    God must feel
    terribly lonely then, too.

Where would you look for God?

God is between us, all around us, within us.

Play a game of hide and seek with a twist: one person hides, and everyone
goes looking for her/him. Each person who finds her/him stays in the hiding
place. Eventually, everyone is "found" together.

I "find" God in _____

I "see" God in _____

AVE THE ENVIRONMENT

I wonder if God has eyes.
If so, they must be just like my teacher's.
They see when people are sad or happy.

If you saw the world through God's eyes, what would you see?

Sometimes my parents tell me to eat more green vegetables and fewer jelly beans!

Maybe they are right, but I still like pink lemonade jelly beans the best.

I wonder if God likes to play. Sometimes grown-ups don't want to play because they are too busy or too tired.
I think that makes God sad.
I think God likes me to play.

Who is in your favorite playground?

How do you play in God's playground?

If I saw the world through God's eyes, I would see _____

_____

_____

_____

Lie down on a big sheet of paper (you might have to tape some sheets of paper together). Have someone trace around your body with a pencil. Finish the drawing of yourself with markers or crayons; cut it out and put it on the wall, or give it to someone you love.

3

Often we find God in other people.
When we do something loving for another person, it's like we're seeing God.
We can be God's paintbrushes by coloring the world with God's love.

Sometimes I like to play
hide and seek with my friends.
We count to ten
and then start looking.
But today my friends
got tired of looking,
and went away before
they found me.
    I felt very lonely.

On Monday, I broke my Mom's vase.
I was scared.
I hid behind the large sofa
in our living room.
Mom came home.
I was glad when she found me.
    I felt lonely all by myself.

Sometimes I think God hides,
and we don't want to look for God,
because we are too busy or too afraid.

    God must feel
    terribly lonely then, too.

Where would you look for God?

God is between us, all around us, within us.

Play a game of hide and seek with a twist: one person hides, and everyone goes looking for her/him. Each person who finds her/him stays in the hiding place. Eventually, everyone is "found" together.

I "find" God in _____

I "see" God in _____

I wonder if God has eyes.
If so, they must be just like my teacher's.
They see when people are sad or happy.

If you saw the world through God's eyes, what would you see?

Sometimes my parents tell me to eat more green vegetables and fewer jelly beans!

Maybe they are right, but I still like pink lemonade jelly beans the best.

I wonder if God likes to play. Sometimes grown-ups don't want to play because they are too busy or too tired.
I think that makes God sad.
I think God likes me to play.

Who is in your favorite playground?

How do you play in God's playground?

If I saw the world through God's eyes, I would see _____

_____

_____

_____

 Lie down on a big sheet of paper (you might have to tape some sheets of paper together). Have someone trace around your body with a pencil. Finish the drawing of yourself with markers or crayons; cut it out and put it on the wall, or give it to someone you love.

Often we find God in other people.
When we do something loving for another person, it's like we're seeing God.
We can be God's paintbrushes by coloring the world with God's love.

Sometimes I like to play
hide and seek with my friends.
We count to ten
and then start looking.
But today my friends
got tired of looking,
and went away before
they found me.
    I felt very lonely.

On Monday, I broke my Mom's vase.
I was scared.
I hid behind the large sofa
in our living room.
Mom came home.
I was glad when she found me.
    I felt lonely all by myself.

Sometimes I think God hides,
and we don't want to look for God,
because we are too busy or too afraid.

    God must feel
    terribly lonely then, too.

Where would you look for God?

God is between us, all around us, within us.

Play a game of hide and seek with a twist: one person hides, and everyone goes looking for her/him. Each person who finds her/him stays in the hiding place. Eventually, everyone is "found" together.

I "find" God in _____

I "see" God in _____

I wonder if God has eyes.
If so, they must be just like my teacher's.
They see when people are sad or happy.

If you saw the world through God's eyes, what would you see?

Sometimes my parents tell me
to eat more green vegetables
and fewer jelly beans!

Maybe they are right, but I still like
pink lemonade jelly beans the best.

I wonder if God likes to play.
Sometimes grown-ups don't want
to play because they are too busy
or too tired.
I think that makes God sad.
I think God likes me to play.

Who is in your favorite playground?

How do you play in God's playground?

If I saw the world through God's eyes, I would see _____

_____

_____

_____

Lie down on a big sheet of paper (you might have to tape some sheets of paper together). Have someone trace around your body with a pencil. Finish the drawing of yourself with markers or crayons; cut it out and put it on the wall, or give it to someone you love.

3

Often we find God in other people.
When we do something loving for another person, it's like we're seeing God.
We can be God's paintbrushes by coloring the world with God's love.

Sometimes I like to play
hide and seek with my friends.
We count to ten
and then start looking.
But today my friends
got tired of looking,
and went away before
they found me.
        I felt very lonely.

On Monday, I broke my Mom's vase.
I was scared.
I hid behind the large sofa
in our living room.
Mom came home.
I was glad when she found me.
        I felt lonely all by myself.

Sometimes I think God hides,
and we don't want to look for God,
because we are too busy or too afraid.

        God must feel
        terribly lonely then, too.

Where would you look for God?

God is between us, all around us, within us.

Play a game of hide and seek with a twist: one person hides, and everyone goes looking for her/him. Each person who finds her/him stays in the hiding place. Eventually, everyone is "found" together.

I "find" God in _____

I "see" God in _____